How to Play the Outfield

MAJOR LEAGUE BASEBALL
MLB

MAJOR LEAGUE
BASEBALL
PLAYERS GUIDES

How to Play the Outfield

Tommie Agee
Jesus Alou
Bill Conigliaro
Willie Davis
Ralph Garr
Reggie Jackson
Al Kaline
Bobby Murcer
Tony Oliva
Amos Otis
Frank Robinson
Pete Rose
Frank Robinson
Pete Rose
Willie Stargell
Rusty Staub
Cesar Tovar

GROSSET & DUNLAP   A NATIONAL GENERAL COMPANY
Publishers   New York

Contents

How to Play the Outfield

Playing the Outfield

You MAY have heard it said that anyone who can catch a ball can play the outfield—as long as he can hit. Don't you believe it! There is a great deal to learn about playing the outfield. And if a young man does not learn it, he is going to have to carry the mightiest bat in the league to hang on to his job. Even then, he may wind up just a pinch-hitter.

Poor outfield play can lose baseball games faster than long hits can win them. And good outfield play can win ball games too, just as long hits can.

An outfielder, of course, must catch fly balls. But in order to catch enough of them to count he must learn to run on his toes, because if he runs on his heels, each step jars his spine and brings a blurring of the vision that can cause him to misjudge a fly ball badly. Take careful note of how you use your feet when you run. If you land on your heel as you jog along, start right away to get out of that habit. Get up on the balls of your feet and run that way all the time. You will run faster like that, anyway, and it will get you in the habit of staying "on your toes."

An outfielder is always running. If he is not chasing a fly ball or running to block a line drive or hard ground ball, he is running to help one of the other fielders—backing him up, in case the ball gets by, or getting close to him in case the ball is dropped. Sometimes you may even have to get close to do the throwing for a fielder who has an injured arm. And you should always *run* to and from your position.

Shoes therefore are important to an outfielder and he should take care that they are always in good

An outfielder must run on his toes.

shape, that they fit him snugly, that the spike plates are not loose or about to become loose, and that the shoes are not likely to split open or fall apart. It is best to have two pairs, one to practice in and one to play in. Because baseball shoes usually stretch from wear, it is a good idea to buy shoes just a bit smaller than your dress shoe size and break them in well before using them in a game.

Find a glove that you can use comfortably. Do not buy one just because it carries the name of a favorite fielder. He may have larger hands than you. You want one that you can carry on your hand easily and use as if it were an extension of your own fingers. Don't mess it up with a lot of oil and goo. Good gloves are all properly treated before you buy them and need no saddle-soap or other extra application.

Fly Balls

Then, when you have yourself properly outfitted, get all the practice you can at catching fly balls. Practice as much as possible catching in a regular outfield with balls hit off a bat from the plate or the plate area. You will find that the fly balls that come straight at you are often the most difficult to deal with because it is hard to judge their carry. A ball may look as if it is going to drop in front of you and just as you start in, it will seem to rise up and sail over your head. It takes a lot of practice to recognize the probable trajectory of balls like this.

12

Practice is the only way to learn to recognize the trajectory of balls hit directly at you.

Many outfielders instinctively start back on a well-hit ball.

Many fielders react instinctively to the sound the bat makes as it strikes the ball. The solid ringing whack that comes when the good wood hits the ball square on warns them that the ball is going to travel a long way and they instinctively start to move toward the fence. Conversely, the relatively dull sound of a bat that has undercut the ball and popped it in a high arc indicates to them that the ball is going to drop short, and they start immediately toward the diamond.

But no one can teach you these things. You have to catch batted balls by the dozen, even the hundred, before you begin to recognize the probable course a ball will take.

As often as possible, you will catch a ball with both hands, trapping it in the glove and getting the bare hand over it at once so you can be sure it will not spin or bounce free and so you will be ready to get off a throw in an instant. There will of course, be many balls that you will have to strain to get to, and these you may be lucky to catch in your glove alone. If you have confidence in your ability to catch a ball, you will be surprised at how many "impossible" catches you can make.

Never give up on a ball until you *know* it is going to go out of the park or hit the wall. And there will be many times when you can go to the wall for a ball and still catch it. After you have developed your judgment in such matters, you will know when to back away from the wall and play the rebound. But in the beginning, and until you learn how to judge the trajectory of a batted ball quickly, go ahead and chase them all. You have to be wrong a great many times before you are right.

Acquaint yourself, however, with the position of the fences and the stands before you start to play in any outfield. Major league parks all have "warning" tracks of cinder-like substance in front of the outfield fences, so the fielder will know of the nearness of the wall without having to take his eye off the ball. But where there is no such track, you should look all around you each time you position yourself and be positive you know just what and where the obstructions are.

When you have developed the savvy necessary to judge the flight of a ball—and this will not take you long if you work at it steadily—you can begin to "play the wall" on the long high drives. Bear in mind that a ball will rebound from a wall at the same angle it approaches it, provided the wall is flat and hard. So you do not run straight at the spot where the ball is going to hit. Instead, you back off and look for the ball to come back toward you at whatever angle it made with the wall coming in. Think of the manner in which a billiard ball rebounds from a cushion. If you send it straight at the cushion, it comes straight back. If you angle it toward the cushion from your right hand, it will angle back to the left in the same degree. A baseball acts the same way.

16

Your home field, however, may have special corners and curves in it that need study. Put in some time every day having someone knock balls against these difficult spots until you learn how a ball behaves when it hits them. Time spent studying rebounds is one way to turn yourself into a real outfielder who can dog a ball down quickly and recover it in time to keep the runner from an extra base.

The Positions

Center field is the most demanding position because there is more territory to cover. The center fielder usually has first call on balls that are hit to his right or left, because he can so often get a better line on them. Line drives to center field are difficult to judge because they often keep rising as they approach the fielder.

In right and left field, however, there are special problems. There are walls or fences to one side as well as behind the fielder and he has to make far more sudden stops than the center fielder. Perhaps the fastest outfielder, and the one with the strongest arm and the most experience, should play center field. But the right fielder, who often has to try to cut a runner down at third base, needs a mighty arm, too.

But no position in the field offers a rest cure, because the fielders have to move fast on almost every ball hit out on the grass. While the teamwork required in the outfield is not so intricate as that needed in the infield, it is still necessary that the fielders help each other.

First of all, they must *talk* to each other. The center fielder may look as if he has the best shot at a fly ball that is going between the fielders. But that does not mean that the other fielder who is close to it simply gives up. He moves toward the ball swiftly, just the same. And if he is going to be in a better position to get off a throw, then he should yell for the ball—and yell loud, and keep on yelling until he hears the other guy tell him to take it.

Even if the center fielder calls him off, he should still range as close to the ball as he can get without interfering with the other man. Then if the catch is missed, he may be able to recover it more quickly than the man who missed it. Or he may even be able to grab a ball that is deflected by the other fellow's glove.

The best place to catch a ball is at shoulder height or higher because that puts you into throwing position most quickly. And catching a ball high sometimes means that, if it does pop out of the glove, you have a chance to grab it again before it hits the ground. Still, many great fielders have caught balls waist-high, because that seemed more natural to them. Perhaps, if you have already devel-

18

Catch the ball high. You may get a second chance at it if it bounces out of your glove.

oped skill at judging and catching balls, you should stick to the method you find easiest. But if you are just beginning your practice, try to make a habit of catching the ball high.

When coming in on a fly ball, it is sometimes necessary to catch the ball low.

While the best practice at catching fly balls is the practice you get during batting drills, when pitched balls are hit to the outfield, fungo hitting is necessary to give you practice at overcoming special

20

weaknesses. A pitched ball hit to the outfield acts very differently from a fungo hit, is harder to catch, and often approaches at greater speed. But a center fielder especially needs lots and lots of fungoes to give him practice at going back for a ball.

As a matter of fact, any outfielder can use this practice. You should station yourself in fairly short outfield and have someone hit fly balls over your head, so that you have to turn and go after them. In chasing a fly ball that is hit over your head, you must turn your back on the plate immediately. The worst way to try to catch a fly ball is by back-pedalling. But if you will turn and run back, with your eye on the ball, you may be surprised at how easy it is to pluck that ball out of the air with your glove. It takes confidence, and confidence comes with practice. Once in a great while a really hard-hit ball may be so far beyond you that all you can do is guess where it may come down and then turn and sprint for that spot. But if you learn, by practice, how to get a quick start on a ball—that is, if you develop judgment as to how far a ball is going to carry, and can start at the crack of the bat—you can often pull down a ball that is hit well beyond you. You do not need to watch your footing because outfields are smooth and clear of obstacles. You can keep your eye right on the ball all the way.

If you are playing a man deep you can occasionally pick a fly ball off the wall or grab it before it goes into the stands. But you also have the problem

If you get a quick start, and keep your eye on the ball all the way, you can sometimes pull down a ball hit well beyond you.

of running in fast on a ball that is going to drop in front of you. And you have to decide sometimes in a half second whether to shoe-string such a ball—that is, try to catch it at the very last instant before it hits the grass—or to stop and take it on the bounce.

In making such a decision you have to use common sense. A missed shoe-string catch can turn a single into a triple, and if there are runners on base with two out, it can bring all the runners home. But there are times when only a daring catch will keep the winning run from crossing the plate. Then, if you have plenty of confidence in your ability to reach the ball and hang on to it, you have to take the chance.

Ground Balls

Every ground ball that comes to the outfield must be charged. If you wait for it to get to you, the runner will be taking extra bases. You will have to decide, from the power with which the ball was hit and the importance of getting a throw off fast, whether to field the ball infield-style, in your natural stride, or to block the ball to make extra sure it does not get by. When runners are not advancing and you get to the ball quickly, and it is hit hard, your best bet will be to block the ball by going to one knee

When runners are advancing, it is best to get down on one knee and block the ball.

and closing off the path of the ball completely.

But many times you will want to get the ball back quickly to keep runners from taking extra bases. Then you will have to field the ball in stride, in front of your forward foot. When you do that, be *sure* you bend your back and get your head over the ball. Most of the time, when a ball gets by, it gets under the glove. So you must be sure to field it with bent knees and bent back, and the hands right on the ground. Get your head down so you can see the underside of the bill of your cap. When you straighten up to throw, you may have to take an extra hop to get into throwing position. And you must know where you are going to throw.

Every outfielder must expect every batted ball to come to him. You should tell yourself before the pitch just what you are going to do with the ball when you get it. The general idea is to throw the ball ahead of the runner. That is, if there is no one on base and you have fielded a ground ball in front of you, you will throw to second base. Be sure there is someone there to throw to and fire the ball in fast and low, so it will bounce to the baseman.

If you field the ball far out on the grass, you must look for the relay man. He will be waving his arms above his head, part way out on the grass. Send the ball to him on the fly, hard and fast. Even though you may sometimes field a ball in infield style, you do not throw that way. Do not snap your throws. Give them the full length of your arm, with a full stride as you let go.

Any throw across the diamond, especially if you are throwing to home, must come in at shoulder height, so that it can be cut off. Do not try to show off your arm by heaving the ball in a high arc so it will go all the way without a bounce. The cut-off man is inside the diamond to pick the throw off when the catcher tells him to, and your throw must

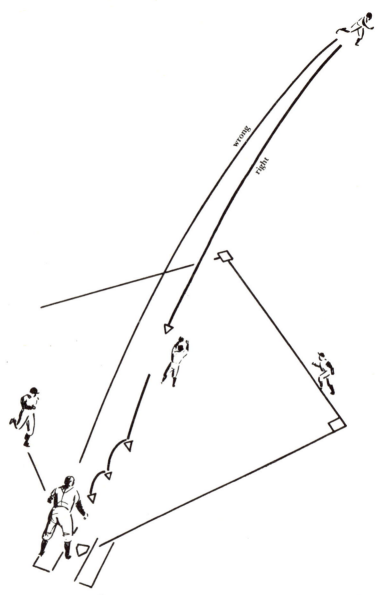

wrong

right

All throws from the outfield should be low enough for a cut-off man to handle if necessary.

be low enough so he can handle it.

Once in a great while, if you have a strong arm and an accurate throw, and the runner is not alert, you can fool him by throwing behind him. You do not do that when there is another runner ahead of him in scoring position. But sometimes a runner will make a lazy turn at a base, or will assume your throw is coming to the base ahead of him and will go a few strides toward the next base, hoping for a bad throw. Then if the ball comes in hard and fast behind him, you will trap him on the baseline. But to make that play, you have to own an exceptional arm because the throw must hit the bull's eye and it must really sizzle.

A medium short fly ball with a man on third often means a try for home by the runner. Sometimes the runner will bluff a run to draw the throw. But don't you bluff a throw, for that will give a smart base runner just that extra split second he needs to score on you. Get the ball back fast and if there is any indication the runner is trying to score, fire the ball to the plate.

When there is a runner on first base and the ball is hit in front of you, for a safe hit, you will usually be trying to get the runner at third, or throwing to keep him from going to third. But do not make such a play automatically. If there are two out when the hit is made, or if the hit-and-run is on, the man on first is going to be off at the sound of the bat and will be aiming for home. Think of this as you field

27

the ball and look for the runner trying for home. Then get the ball in there ahead of him. Of course if it was a hard-hit ball, and you fielded it deep, you will be throwing to the relay man. But *know,* before the play develops, what you are going to do. And do not throw blindly to cut off a run if the man has got a good start and is bound to score. A man on second, with a well-hit ball, may be too far gone for you to catch when you field the ball. But if you get your throw in fast and hard to second base, you may be able to nail the man who hit the ball and thus choke off the start of a rally. This is a possibility you should also have in mind as you expect the ball to come your way. Consider the speed of the runner, the depth at which you field the ball, and the tactical situation. If you know that runner is going to score, then throw the ball to second base—fast.

Strategy

Of course, you must always be working with your pitcher, to help him with what he is trying to do. If there is a runner at second base with nobody out, the pitcher will be trying to keep the batter from hitting into the hole between first and second. If the batter is a left-handed pull hitter, the pitcher will be throwing him outside pitches, and so he will not be able to pull with his full power. That means that if you are in right field you will not be playing quite so deep as if you were defending against his power. Instead you will be playing somewhat shorter to field a possible ground ball and get a hard throw off to third base.

If the batter is a man who likes to hit to the "opposite" field (left-hander to left field, right-hander to right), play him so that he will have to hit the ball over your head to get a base hit. The chances will be very much in your favor that he will not be able to do so, or that he will get the ball up high enough so you can catch it.

Bear in mind that a runner can score from third base after a caught *foul* fly, with less than two out. If a foul fly comes your way with a runner on third, let it drop, unless it is a short one that you can catch while facing the diamond. If the man on third represents the winning run (less than two out, score tied, the other club at home, final inning) take no chances on a foul fly.

It is also good to bear in mind that in the situation just described (winning run on third), a *long* fly ball is going to win the game whether it is caught or allowed to drop. So what you must guard against are the short flies, the line drives, and the bloop hits. Therefore you move in toward the diamond to make any catches in close.

You should try for all short flies, unless called off them. Because the outfielder is facing the diamond he is almost always in a better position to make a throw than an infielder, who will have to turn his back on the diamond to follow the ball.

But remember the need for teamwork at all times. Shout your intentions. Let your teammates all hear you: "I've got it! I've got it!" But stay clear if another man has called for it, and tell him: "Take it!" He will not be shouting unless he has a good line on the ball.

As a matter of fact, you should always be in position to play the ball, to back up throws, to assist another outfielder. The outfield is no place to concentrate on getting a sunburn or to think about your next time at bat. Get your weight forward, on the balls of your feet, hands on knees, ready to explode in the direction of the ball. On throws from inside the diamond, to any base, move in to back up the infielder. When there is a rundown in progress, move toward the diamond to help out. When there is a base uncovered with runners on base, *cover* it!

While you do not need to watch your feet as you run after a ball, and can take for granted that your pathway will be smooth, there are certain hazards in the outfield you must always be aware of. Sun, wind, and fences or stands can all affect your fielding. As soon as you get out in your position, check the wind direction and be sure you know where the sun is. If it is a partly cloudy day, be sure you know where the sun is likely to appear. Be ready to make allowances for the wind on long fly balls. It may hold up hits that would otherwise go over the fence or hit it. It may move the ball to right or left, or give it more carry. In allowing for the wind, try to place yourself so that the wind brings the ball to you.

You will of course always have your sunglasses in your cap and be ready to flip them into position whenever a ball seems headed into the sun. But sunglasses will not eradicate the sun's glare when you are looking directly into it. Still, you should never "surrender" to the sun. There is always some way of getting a glimpse of the ball. One way is to glance up at it sideways, so that you do not get the sun straight on. Or you should look away from the sun and try to judge where the ball will reappear. A big-league outfielder does not throw his arms over his face and duck just because a ball goes into the sun. He keeps trying to get a sight on the ball from other angles, and is always prepared to catch the ball.

Of course every ball hit to the outfield must be thrown back fast into the diamond. Never lob balls back or hang on to them. Make a habit of quick, low returns. You will notice that you get a stronger throw when you are moving toward the diamond. Sometimes you may have to hop into throwing position to get your full strength into your throw. And when you are handling a routine fly ball, it is a good idea to give yourself a little extra room, moving back away from the spot where you will make the catch, and then taking the ball on the move, so you can get off a quick powerful throw without an extra wind-up or hop. This is the mark of an experienced outfielder, his taking fly balls on the move, instead of standing rooted to the spot and then having to go through extra motions to get full strength into the throw.

High fly balls that come down close to high stands often get into a backdraft that causes them to drift into the field, so if you get too close to a stand on such a ball, you may suddenly find the ball is swooping off behind you. Make allowances for this when you are playing close to a high stand —as in right or left field and on high fouls—and do not get too close. Remember it is easier to reach out than to back up. Outfielders have to learn to play position on batters. Managers will often signal outfielders where to play on certain batters or in certain situations. But you should not rely on someone else to tell you every time how to position yourself. You can make a study of opposing batters in batting practice, noting which ones are the long ball hitters, which ones like to pull the ball, which batters take a short grip on the bat and try to place their hits.

Naturally, you will play the long ball hitters more deeply than the spray hitters. And you will, in general, play left-handed hitters to hit to right and right-handers to hit to left. But there are always exceptions and variations. The pull hitter who must be played against the fence and near the foul line in right (he being a left-hander) may also have a habit of slicing outside pitches close to the foul

All balls hit to the outfield should be fired back into the infield immediately. Do not lob them or hang onto them.

line in *left*. The left fielder, then, while playing to make the man hit over his head, may also play closer than normal to the foul line, giving the batter a big "hole" in left-center—where it is presumed he cannot hit with any power.

You also have to position yourself or move according to what your pitcher is doing. If he likes to work close to right-handed batters and outside to left-handed batters, then the left fielders will probably play relatively close to the foul line with every batter, although he will play shorter on the left-handers.

An infielder, most likely the shortstop, should pass on to the outfield a sign to show what pitch is coming. Curve balls are far easier to pull than fast balls. Pitchers do not like to have fielders move too soon, and thus give away the pitch. But you should be ready to take off in the direction where the ball is likely to fall, depending on whether it is a fast ball or curve. The sign will be given by the shortstop behind his back and the outfielders should watch for it and make sure that every fielder has it. Knuckleball pitchers get a lot of "opposite-field" hits, because the batter usually swings late and swings from an open stance. Take this into account as you take your position in the field or prepare to move with the pitch.

The greatest of center fielders have been the men who can "go back" best and who also charge ground balls hard and field them quickly. They thus become "fifth infielders," for they are able to play so close behind second base that they have actually been known to make put-outs there, and they can catch balls on the fly that would normally have to be chased by an infielder. To play in this manner

34

requires not only tremendous speed but an ability to judge batted balls that amounts to instinct. It is of course an automatic reaction that comes from many, many hours of patient practice. If you can find a fungo hitter willing to give you long daily practice at "going back" on balls hit over your head, and if you are a really fast runner, with something like record speed in the dash, then you may be able to play this way. **1772580**

If you have a mighty arm and the courage to play close to the wall, you may do best in right, where the fielder has to haul down long drives and also field shorter hits and uncork fast hard throws to third base that will still come in low enough to be cut off when necessary.

A mighty arm, however, is nothing to be toyed with. An outfielder should take good care of his throwing arm. That does not mean avoiding long throws, for if you do not work your arm out good and hard ever day it may deteriorate. It means throwing hard only after the arm is properly warmed up by a dozen or more easy short throws. And it means throwing *overhand,* with the full length of the arm, and a full stride toward the target.

Running and throwing every day should be routine with an outfielder. He should never get into a game until after he has the sweat started with a good run and some easy throwing. Also he should *always* run out to his position and back. No one, and especially no manager, likes to see an outfielder loafing, even if he is just carrying his glove out to work.

Staying in Condition

MERELY playing an occasional game of baseball will not keep you in top physical condition—the kind of condition you must be in to play at the top of your form. If you are going to be a baseball player, you must be prepared to throw hard, with your full strength, to run at top speed around the bases or in the field, to withstand bumps and bruises, to react swiftly, to bend down low, straighten up quickly, and maintain your balance.

Many people imagine that such abilities come naturally—that you have "quick reflexes" by nature, or good natural balance, or great strength or speed or agility, or that you just naturally recover quickly from injury.

It is true, of course, that you do have certain natural physical gifts. But if you do not work hard at developing and conserving them, they can wither away in a fairly short span of years. Being in good shape does more for you than just enabling you to run faster and farther without getting winded. It can give you unexpected strength and stamina when you need it. It can actually help you recover more quickly from sprains, strains, bruises, bumps and cuts, sharpen your eye, improve your timing, and speed up your reactions. The "bright eye" that is often a mark of the well-conditioned athlete is really bright, in the sense that it accommodates more quickly and registers more definitely. The "tone" that can give you a glowing appearance and a feeling of internal well-being is more than psychological. Well-conditioned muscles really are stronger, more supple, less inclined to tear or bruise.

But before you set out on a regimen of training, you should remind yourself that training does not mean *straining*. Regular, demanding exercise is necessary. But do not get the idea that if a little exercise is good, ten times as much is ten times better. The body must be brought around slowly. You cannot make up for weeks of inactivity with one day of strenuous effort.

Then too, you must be sure you are really physically able to give your body the kind of workout you are planning. If there is any doubt about your organic or muscular stamina, you should check with your doctor *before* you start. Do not wait to find out if something will go wrong.

Most healthy bodies can stand a good deal of punishment and there will always be soreness and stiffness after a workout following a long layoff. Do not give in to mere aches of this sort. Just make sure in advance that you have no organic or muscular disability. Then stick religiously to a program of exercise.

Of course, to play ball you want to exercise the muscles and develop the skills you will use on the diamond. But even when you do not have room to run and bat and throw, or lack the facilities, there are other things you can do to develop the proper muscles. There is just one form of exercise that does not seem suited to a ball player, and that is weight-lifting. The oversize, bunchy muscles that are developed in this work do not seem to lend themselves to the demands that ball-playing makes. For throwing and batting and fielding and baserunning, the athlete needs the long supple muscles that come from steady exercise rather than strain.

Swimming is excellent for developing muscles of this sort, especially in the shoulders and arms. The throwing muscles can be worked into shape by pulling on a lightly weighted pulley—the "chest-weights" that can be found in most gymnasiums. And of course the legs can be strengthened by running and climbing.

The best place to run, of course, is outdoors, if you are situated where this is possible—near a park or some other open space where you can keep running

38

for a long time without dodging traffic or waiting for lights. If you cannot find room for running out-doors every day, then run indoors and run regularly. "Running in place"—that is, lifting the knees in a running motion without going anywhere—is not the same as running unless you actually thrust all your weight into the air with each step. Just lifting the knees up and down is not the sort of workout you need. But if you can actually jump into the air off one foot and then the other, you will achieve the effect of running. Straddle hops or jumping rope will also give you the right sort of workout, with the added advantage that rope jumping increases your agility.

But do not take exercise of this sort lightly. Of course you will work into it gradually, doing a bit more each day until you improve your capacity and can actually feel the *bite* of the exercise—the heavy breathing and the pouring sweat that indicates you are really extending yourself. When you find that the work-out begins to come easy and does not make you pant and sweat as it did, add more work. Then, when the exercise is over, flop somewhere and get your wind back. Complete effort and com-plete rest add stamina to your muscles—even to the heart muscle.

There are many other exercises you can find or even invent to work out all the joints and muscles you are going to use. If you can find ways of imi-tating the actual moves you will have to make in playing ball, you will be sure to add strength and agility in the right spots. For instance, in a restricted space, you can field imaginary bunts, hopping about in a circle as you bend your knees and your back to pick up the imaginary ball, then straighten to throw it. You may have to work hard to get into the habit of *bending*. Some young people will bend their knees and try to field the ball with a straight back. Or they will bend over at the hips and forget to bend the knees. Just remember that baseball is played in the dirt and you must get right down there to field a ball. Bend *low* each time, with your tail down and your head bent right over the imaginary ball. Keep this up until you are really winded.

Strong fingers and a strong grip are needed for hard throws. The fingers are easy to exercise. Just a rubber ball or a spring device you can carry in your pocket will give you a chance to work out your fingers at almost any time.

But there are specific exercises you can add to your program that will also help strengthen the proper muscles. One of the toughest and most productive is the push-up. This is a familiar exercise to anyone who has ever done gym work—stretching full length, with knees straight, supporting yourself on toes and hands, with your tail flat, then lowering yourself until you touch your chest to the floor without letting your weight drop to the floor, then pushing yourself back into position again. If you

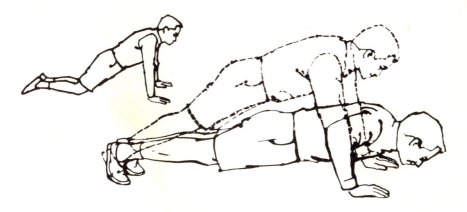

Regular push-up.

are in good shape you can probably do fifty or more of these before you begin to flag. But now try it on your extended fingers! Plant finger and thumb-tips on the floor and move your weight slowly up and down that way. Easy? Now try it without your thumb. Now try it on two fingers. When you can do a bunch of push-ups that way, you will really be building strength in hands and forearms.

But actual throwing motions, even if you have no ball to throw, will help too. The motion used in punching a bag is much like the throwing motion and uses the same muscles. And if you have no bag to punch you can shadow-box—punching the air as you shuffle around the room.

Most exercise that does you good however is a working against resistance of some sort. While this can be overdone and result in strain if you try such

Fingertip push-up.

stunts as lifting the front end of an automobile, you can get good out of it if you are sensible. For instance, a cheap and easy apparatus to set up in cellar, garage, back-yard, or alleyway is an old spare tire hanging on a heavy rope. You can mark a spot on the tire about the size of a baseball and then wallop it with a baseball bat. As hitting the heavy bag gives extra force to a boxer's punch, walloping the tire this way will strengthen your hitting muscles. It will also give you a chance to practice your swing and help you get into the habit of sighting the target (the ball) as you swing.

But you need no extra apparatus to practice your swing. You can do this anywhere, as long as there is no danger of breaking any furniture with the bat. You do not even need a regular bat to practice with. And you can stand in front of a mirror (far enough away so as not to hit it) as you go through your swing, to make sure you are getting your elbows away from your body, are drawing back as you start your swing and are following through properly. You can also get good practice in limited space by hitting one of those plastic "whiffle balls." This sort of workout does not take the place of batting practice. But it does help you loosen and strengthen your batting muscles and improve your batting eye.

Rope climbing or climbing of any sort that involves your hands and arms can also give you a good workout and improve muscles in shoulder, wrist, and hand. Or just plain work with the hands —hammering, shoveling, digging, sawing, chopping, hoeing—if you do a lot of it and do it steadily, will strengthen you in all the right places. As a matter of fact, because the use of a baseball bat is much like the use of a heavy hammer or axe, this sort of work is particularly valuable to a ballplayer.

On days and in places where it is not possible to get in a lot of running, you can still give your leg and calf muscles a good workout by climbing stairs on your toes, or, to be more exact, on the balls of your feet. Press down hard on each step. Keep your back straight, pull your stomach in. This will give you a simple workout and will also give you extra practice at staying "on your toes."

Another good exercise is the toe-stand. You stand flat-footed and simply bob up onto your toes as far as you can go. Do it either one foot at a time or with

43

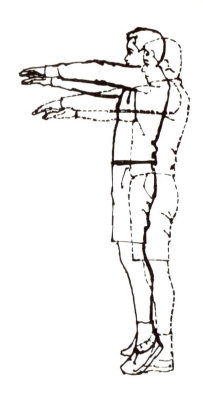

Toe-stand.

both feet at once. You can use a support at first, but later you'll want to do toe-stands unsupported, to train your balance.

This business of staying on your toes is of great importance. A catcher must keep his weight on the balls of his feet as he crouches, as he receives the pitch, as he moves out after a bunt. Only if you are in the habit of doing this will you have the agility you need to hop quickly into throwing position. A

44

baserunner must run on his toes, too, and he must have his weight there as he leads off a base. An outfielder must run on his toes or his vision will be blurred as he pounds along. An infielder must stay on his toes, with his weight forward or he will not get a proper jump on a ground ball. A pitcher must push off with his toes and ideally land on his toes to get full strength into his pitch and hold his balance as he delivers the ball.

So you need all the practice you can get at moving around on your toes. Climbing stairs, and making a workout of it, helps you in that way. Skipping rope also helps. And if you take care to do *all* your running on your toes, you will be getting your body into the right habit.

For some reason or other, many young fellows seem to have most trouble in bending their knees, to squat low or to jump high. So if you will take a certain time each day to do deep knee-bends—in which you stand on the balls of your feet with arms outspread and let yourself down on your haunches and back up again *slowly*—you will help overcome this weakness. Remind yourself every time you bend down, whether to pick something off the floor or to lift something, to bend your knees as well as your back. And try jumping over low obstacles by bending the knees and hopping over with feet together, again and again.

In all exercise—not merely in throwing—you should do a short warm-up before going at it full

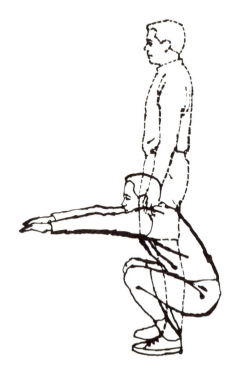

Deep knee-bend.

strength. Muscles are less likely to suffer pulls and strains if the blood is circulating in them. An easy trot or a gentle beating of the arms across the chest will speed up circulation enough to get blood into all the big muscles. Never put sudden strain on a cold muscle. And remember a muscle can be "cold"—that is, without a full supply of blood— even on the hottest day of the year.

Other good warmup exercises are toe-touching, a great lower-back and hamstring stretcher; trunk-

46

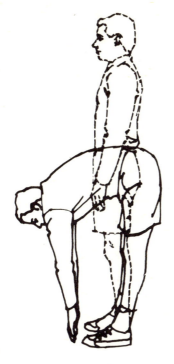

Toe-touching.

bending, not only a good rib or intercostal muscle stretcher, but a means to eliminate any spare tire around your middle you may have picked up during the off-season; and torso-twisting, which also prevents stiffness and helps slim down your middle.

During the season, you can shorten your exercise period on days when you play a full game—and if you are a pitcher, you can cut it out (except for warm-ups) altogether on the day you pitch. Off-season, you should make a religion of your daily

Trunk-bending.

workout. And even when you are playing ball, you can still find time to practice your swing and loosen up your throwing muscles. Set yourself a regular regime to follow—so many push-ups, so many straddle-hops, so many deep knee-bends or walking in a squat for a certain time, so many rope-skips, and a certain distance to run. If you live in a cold climate, you can substitute skating for running. And swimming can take the place of arm exercises. But the *regular* performance of these tasks is what

48

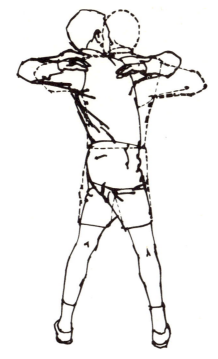

Torso-twisting.

counts. If you miss three days, you cannot hope to make them all up by doing three times as much in one day. As a matter of fact, if you lay off too long, you may find you have to start in gradually and work up to your peak again.

But you should give yourself regular days off too. A complete rest—no warm-up, no run, no throwing, no bending—does the body good at intervals. Just do not let your days off come all in a row or you will throw away the benefit of regular exercise.

Other Sports

Most baseball players play other games too at different seasons. But if your chief interest is playing ball, you have to give precedence to that and avoid the pastimes that can unfit you for baseball. Golf usually helps a ballplayer, for it involves hitting a ball, keeping the eye on the ball, and hiking long distances. But basketball has its dangers. You may start to play without sufficient practice in the special moves the new game requires. And sudden stops and turns in shoes that do not slide may give you a knee-twist that can bedevil you in your baseball playing. So if you go in for this game—and many great ballplayers have—make sure that you get plenty of preliminary practice to accustom your muscles to the new tasks.

Touch football is great for wind and stamina. But tackle or touch-tackle carries a real danger of a wrenched or separated shoulder. Trying to stop a flying ball-carrier with an outstretched arm can put you on the shelf for a whole baseball season.

Swimming, as we have said, is great preparation, even better than golf. And running, either dash or long distance, will do you nothing but good.

Of course, if your regular occupation offers you plenty of exercise, you need add to your program only the 'sort of workout you need to develop the muscles you do not use regularly. Deep knee-bends, quick squats, and hops are not usually performed except as deliberate exercises, so you may want to go in for these every day. And running should be part of your program all the time.

Common Sense About Eating

OVER THE YEARS, coaches, trainers, athletes, and faddists have cooked up all sorts of fairy tales about food. For a long time it was taken for granted that a big steak before a ball game made a pitcher or catcher healthy, tough and impervious to injury. Nowadays everyone knows a ballplayer does better on an empty stomach. There have also been "training tables" that offered no fruit lest the "acid" disturb the stomach, no fried food of any sort, and very few sweets. It was almost as if someone had decided any food a man could enjoy could not possibly be good for him. It was also widely believed that certain foods could never be safely combined— that if any milk and any pickled food were consumed at the same meal, for instance, immediate stomach cramps would follow. And dark ale, it was preached, was the drink that really built a man's body.

51

Now we know that a healthy stomach can ingest comfortably almost any edible substance, as long as it is taken in moderate amounts. Fried foods in large quantity can sometimes cause distress, particularly if the cooking is done in grease that has been standing around for a day or two. And highly spiced foods, if consumed in large quantities or on a too-frequent basis, can also cause your stomach to complain and can interfere with your playing ability. But unless you have real stomach woes (and some people do own "nervous stomachs" that have to be treated tenderly), you need not be uneasy about eating what you like as long as you never cram in excess quantities.

Nor should you fret about "vitamins" or try to add to your strength by popping pills every day. If you eat some meat or other protein (cheese or eggs), along with a citrus fruit or green vegetable and some carbohydrate (starch or sweet) at every meal, and add some raw fruit or vegetable for a snack, you are going to get all the vitamins you need. What you should watch out for—because they tend to put extra lard on your frame and so slow you down —are the foods that create their own appetite: sweets and salted or spiced snacks. And if you extend your stomach by over-consumption of carbonated beverages you will begin to have an "empty" feeling even after you have eaten all you need.

In general, however, you just need to be moderate. You can eat what you like and add a few snacks, just as long as you do not begin to gather extra loose flesh around your middle. If you do begin to take on more weight than you should—if your pants get too tight and your shirt collar suddenly grows too small, even though you are all through growing upwards—you can get back to playing weight simply by reducing your intake a little. That is, you can still eat what you like. But just don't eat all you *want*. If you leave the table, after refusing that extra slice, feeling still a little hungry, you can comfort yourself in the knowledge that your body will now begin to feed on that spare tire you may be wearing.

Young players may take on a few extra pounds in the off-season, because they will peel them off when work begins. But never put on more than you know you will take off in the season. If your off-season weight exceeds your playing weight by more than ten pounds, you should cut down on the intake until you get your weight back within bounds.

Pitchers and catchers can afford to carry a *little* extra weight—or can afford to weigh a little more than their ideal weight, because they are almost sure to lose a few pounds in a nine-inning game. But be strict with yourself as to what constitutes your ideal weight. Don't kid yourself about being "naturally" fat. You know if you have flesh around your hips and abdomen that is not made of muscle. Don't let it start to bulge. Being lean and hard may make you theoretically underweight, but if wind, appetite, and stamina remain good, you are better off thin than fat.

The "Good Things" of Life

NO ONE CAN take an interest in professional athletics without becoming aware that there are a certain number of performers who like to live it up in all their off-time, perhaps on the theory that the big money may not last too long—or perhaps even on the theory that it will last forever and so they don't have to fret about tomorrow. And because a few famous athletes of recent days have earned a lot of newspaper, magazine, and book space through their extra-curricular activities, some young fellows begin to believe that this sort of life is what marks the successful athlete.

But study these life-stories sometime and notice the strange parallel between the high living and the excessive number of injuries. Note how often you read that some cocktail-lounge celebrity is also a frequent customer of the team physician, how many times the night-life hero is hobbling around with a cast on his ankle or a half mile of bandage on his frame, a shoulder in a sling, or a knee that needs an operation.

While clean-living athletes do sometimes get hurt, they never post the number of sprains and fractures and muscle tears and plain charley horses that are awarded to the stay-out-all-nights. That is simply because tired muscles cannot withstand sudden strains or extra-long usage the way rested, healthy muscles can. So the boys who spend their stamina riding the night circuit are actually subtracting whole seasons from their careers and may even be heading for a sudden cutting off of the income that makes this supposed "good life" possible. And when the income is gone, the merry friends and companions who add so much to the gayety of these evenings have a way of taking off too.

We might as well be honest and admit that moderate consumption of alcohol does a healthy person no harm and may even do him good, for it does relax tension and dilates constricted blood vessels. And no matter what your Sunday school teacher may tell you, a man can even get high two or three times a year and suffer no ill effects whatever— unless he happens to be one of those poor souls who, once they have experienced that world of alcohol where all fears are diminished and all pains are numbed, just cannot ever face the real world for any extended period again.

But steady and excess consumption of alcoholic drinks will not only add useless fat to your frame (and *all* alcoholic beverages, not just beer, are loaded with calories), it will rob you of rest, slow your reflexes and eat into your stamina. It will also greatly decrease your value to your ballclub and make managers less likely to look for ways to keep you on the roster. There may have been supermen in the past (and most of the stories you read have been grossly exaggerated) who could put away gallons of strong drink and still appear bright-eyed at game time, but there do not seem to be any such in the world today.

Smoking is bad news too, even though it may not have the prompt debilitating effect of excess alcohol. Smoking as a matter of fact has the opposite effect—it constricts the blood vessels and drives up the blood pressure, thus adding to the effect of nervous tension. And anyone who reads the papers or recalls the history of some of the tragic deaths in baseball in the past decade, knows that the long-run effects of smoking can be dire in the extreme.

Moderation in smoking may perhaps lessen the harm, but who knows what "moderation" is, and how many smokers are there who can observe a limit? There used to be a time when lighting up a cigarette or cigar was a sign that a guy had finally become a man. But the time is approaching when this will be more likely to be accepted as the sign of a limited intelligence.

A great many athletes—although not all, by any means—have a tendency to develop nervous symptoms before a game, especially before a crucial game. Pitchers are most often prey to this trouble. And for some reason, a number of people think these symptoms must be promptly "treated," with pills or tranquilizing concoctions of some sort.

But this ailment, if it can be called an ailment, is a good sign. It indicates that the competitive instincts—the basic fears that prompt the sudden flow of juices in the body—are at work. The ductless glands are getting the body ready for a super-effort, pouring in the additives that enable muscles to exert more strength, eyes to see more clearly, reflexes to operate with lightning speed.

So perhaps the sandwich you so foolishly tried to eat before the game does not set well on the stomach. That's nature's way of reminding you to keep you stomach empty so you can travel faster and farther. Perhaps you have to go to the toilet an extra time or two. Again nature is getting the excess weight off the frame. Animals have more sense than to eat when they are in a state of alarm. (Grazing animals, who are in an almost constant state of alarm, have two stomachs—one to store the food in, the other to digest it when the animal is holed up and at rest.)

So this nervousness, no matter how it may rack and annoy you, is not something you want to suppress by medication. It will disappear spontaneously as soon as the muscles get involved in the contest and begin to use up that extra juice.

You have probably noticed how, after an especially exciting and successful effort, you find yourself all charged up, wanting to talk, to shout, to tell someone all about what happened, to pound your mates on the back—to perform a lot of antics that you might never have any urge to perform at normal times. That is the extra juice still working on you, and it is not at all bad. The blood sugar is high, the adrenalin is still flowing, and your system needs a way to keep working it off. Remember it is *good* to be this way. Don't start popping pills to dull this feeling. There may even come times when you have to "psych" yourself to cultivate this feeling.

Your mental attitude is going to have a great deal to do with your success, no matter where you play. The first thing you need is belief in yourself, so that defeat and discouragement, instead of turning you off completely, will only make you angry and more determined. The athlete who tries something and quits when he finds out he cannot do it is no athlete at all.

No one is born with all the skills developed. Determination will enable you to perform tasks that seem far beyond you at the start. Just turn your back on all your failures and dwell on every success, no matter how small. There is hardly a pro athlete alive who has not known failure and frustration. Some have been rejected three and four times or have been dropped to the minors after one season

58

and had to take the slow, difficult pathway back.

Nowadays you hear a lot of people putting down professional athletics because they are not "relevant" or add nothing to the improvement of the human race or some such thing. They may be right. They certainly have a right to think and say that. But if you have any convictions of that sort, you had best stay out of baseball. Baseball is a game that you cannot enjoy, and cannot perform your best in, if you cannot put your whole heart into it.

The half-hearted performer, no matter how talented he may be, is the unhappy athlete—and the short-term athlete, too. Of course, baseball is just a game. It is, like all professional sports, an entertainment, meant to occupy and amuse and excite people who pay to watch it. But it has many characteristics that make it attractive as a profession too—just as attractive as many other businesses and perhaps more attractive than most.

In baseball, a man does not make good on the strength of his connections, his money, his racial or national background, the schools he attended or the handsome face that God awarded him. He gets ahead strictly on his performance. If you can hit big league pitching safely three times out of ten, if you can get big league batters out, if you can call a solid game behind the plate, you are going to find many a handsome payday in professional baseball, even if your grandparents went without shoes and spoke with an accent.

Besides, baseball is the greatest fun game there is to play. It may even "build character," as some school coaches used to say. But it will do nothing for you if it isn't fun. And it won't be fun if you don't put your whole heart into it and play it to win—even when you are ten runs behind!

The
Non-Combatants

SOONER or later, at some level of your participation in organized baseball—whether Little League, scholastic, collegiate, semi-pro, or professional—you are going to be asked, or told, to coach a base or even manage a team. Or you may even find yourself in the position of umpiring a game, in which case you will be surprised to find that you are just about the most important person on the field. (Some players never get over this experience and go on to carve out fine careers for themselves as umpires.) In every case, the basic principles of baseball apply, and what you have learned as a player will be enough to guide you in your new, non-combatant position. But if you wish to refine your abilities, we offer you the following remarks on coaching and umpiring, which have been adapted from *How to Play Winning Baseball.**

Coaching and Signs

John J. McGraw signaled for practically every Giant pitch thrown to the New York Yankees in the 1922 World Series. With great deliberation, he called each delivery to Babe Ruth, who got only two hits in seventeen times at bat, and no home runs.

"My pitchers liked it that way," he explained. "I think players, as a rule, can do a more workmanlike job when they feel that someone else is carrying the responsibility. I gave the signs directly to my catcher, who had to turn around, but I left nothing to chance or relay."

The question of whether this was a good practice or not is answered by the result: The Giants won the Series without a defeat.

Eddie Sawyer, manager of the pennant-winning Phillies in 1950, abandoned the practice of giving signs to his hitters in the Spring of 1951 and "turned his batters loose at the plate." The Phillies slid into the second division in an amazing form reverse, and in mid-1952, the Phillies turned Sawyer loose.

Somewhere between the severe McGraw methods and the unfortunate experiment of Eddie Sawyer is the ideal method of directing a ball club from the bench: Once again it is a matter for individual managers and ball clubs to decide. Regardless, one thing should be understood: If the manager chooses to sign for each pitch and each swing, he should assume complete responsibility for failures as well as victories. Among younger players, coaches and signs should be used principally in emergencies. Giving signs to show authority destroys faith in leadership.

An over-coached team cannot develop spirit and initiative.

Let the players and the team work out their own destiny, and help them only when they get into trouble.

A batter who has hit safely to left- or right-center needs advice from the first base coach on whether to stop or keep going. Give it to him as soon as possible, preferably with arm waving. The voice may be drowned, and a smart first baseman will yell advice contrary to your own.

A runner steaming into third base on the same type of hit wants to know whether to stop or try for the plate. Judge the outfielder's position, his arm and your player's speed. Then make your decision known as quickly as possible. If you have made a wrong decision, don't be afraid to admit it. Passing the buck is the sure way of disrupting team spirit.

The first base coach helps the runner with his lead off first. He must yell information on whether the ball hit is high, low, far or near, and whether or not it will be caught. Make your words clear and not panicky.

The third base coach must watch the long fly ball on a tag-up and yell "Go!" but never an instant before the ball is in the fielder's glove. The umpire stands in front of the runner so that he can watch the catch and quickly switch his gaze to the bag. If he finds that the foot has left the bag before his gaze reaches it, he will allow the fielder's claim that the runner left the bag before the catch. Why gamble on a sure out, when a split-second delay will insure a clean "leave"?

The third base coach advises the runner on second as to lead and the pick-off play.

The first base coach checks signals and, if something goes wrong, he yells a signal or calls for the batter to "step out."

Too many signs on a ball club are worse than none at all.

The over-loaded batter is always looking for changes of "strategy." His batting is affected. The base runner always looking for "strategic" sign-changes is more likely to get caught off base.

Go over the entire opposition thoroughly before the ball game.

The sign for the bunt can easily be given before the batter leaves the bench or the on deck circle. If not, it should be as simple as possible, and always acknowledged by the batter. The same applies to the hit-and-run signals. Changing at the last minute creates unnecessary tension, and fools the opposition far less than it does your own players.

Make up your own signs from a pattern of actions. They will be easier remembered that way.

Any natural movement of the cap, hands, foot, sandwiched in between two other natural actions will do the trick. Don't let the players "put on" too many signs, for the missed sign is a major cause of friction among players, Big League or bush. The manager should take charge, and the coaches should be his lieutenants.

Ten Rules for the Umpire

1. He should know the rules and interpret them with common sense.
2. He should know that there are three appeal plays, ruling only when asked to by the player. They are:
   a. Leaving base before fly ball is caught.
   b. Not touching a base in rounding the turn, or home plate, except in case of a close slide calling for a decision.
   c. Player batting out of turn.
3. He must never call a play or a pitch too soon. Remember that a pitch or a play is nothing until he calls it ball or strike, safe or out. Call it too late, rather than too soon.
4. Call a tipped-bat play as soon as possible and always without delay. Remember that a tipped bat can also hit a triple, which hit is cancelled out by a tipped bat decision, the offended batter

getting only to first base, and a near riot could be expected.

5. Prearranged understandings should be made between plate and base umpire for help in emergency on half-swings, hit batsmen and border-line infield flys.

6. Never reverse your associate umpire. But if a particularly loud protest is made on your own decision, consult your associate and, if you are wrong, don't be afraid of reversing yourself.

7. On the all-important interference plays, do not weigh *intent* to interfere. All that matters is, did the interference take place.

8. Call balks quickly, with both hands raised high, palms forward and moved toward pitcher's box, automatically stopping play.

9. Go over ground rules thoroughly, and permit no "additional rules" that could give either team an advantage during the game.

10. Keep your eye on the baseball, for nothing can happen without it.

The Official Rules

THE FOLLOWING selection from the Official Baseball Rules are applicable to the game in all professional and amateur leagues, with the following exceptions in the Little League: (1) Little League games last six rather than nine innings; (2) the batter cannot run if the catcher drops a third strike; (3) runners may not leave the base until the pitch has reached the batter; and (4) runners are allowed only one base on a pitcher's wild pickoff throw. Matters of organization, equipment, and the playing field are not covered here, since they vary among amateur leagues and must allow for more flexibility than the professional rules admit. This selection is from *Baseball Rules in Pictures*, reprinted with special permission from *Official Baseball Rules*, copyright © 1964 by the Commissioner of Baseball, and is reproduced with permission of the publisher.

2.00—Definitions of Terms.
(All definitions in Rule 2.00 are listed alphabetically.)

ADJUDGED is a judgment decision by the umpire.

An APPEAL is the act of a fielder in claiming violation of the rules by the offensive team.

A BALK is an illegal act by the pitcher with a runner or runners on base, entitling all runners to advance one base.

A BALL is a pitch which does not enter the strike zone in flight and is not struck at by the batter.

A BASE is one of four points which must be touched by a runner in order to score a run; more usually applied to the canvas bags and the rubber plate which mark the base points.

A BASE ON BALLS is an award of first base granted to a batter who, during his time at bat, receives four pitches outside the strike zone.

A BATTER is an offensive player who takes his position in the batter's box.

The BATTER'S BOX is the area within which the batter shall stand during his time at bat.

The BATTERY is the pitcher and catcher.

BENCH OR DUGOUT is the seating facilities reserved for players, substitutes and other team members in uniform when they are not actively engaged on the playing field.

A BUNT is a batted ball not swung at, but intentionally met with the bat and tapped slowly within the infield.

A CALLED GAME is one in which, for any reason, the umpire-in-chief terminates play.

A CATCH is the act of a fielder in getting secure possession in his hand or glove of a ball in flight and firmly holding it; providing he does not use his cap, protector, pocket or any other part of his uniform in getting possession. It is not a catch, however, if simultaneously or immediately following his contact with the ball, he collides with a player, or with a wall, or if he falls down, and as a result of such collision or falling, drops the ball. If the fielder has made the catch and drops the ball while in the act of making a throw following the catch, the ball shall be adjudged to have been caught. In establishing the validity of the catch, the fielder shall hold the ball long enough to prove that he has complete control of the ball and that his release of the ball is voluntary and intentional.

The CATCHER is the fielder who takes his position back of the home base.

The CATCHER'S BOX is that area within which the catcher shall stand until the pitcher delivers the ball.

A COACH is a team member in uniform appointed by the manager to perform such duties as the manager may designate, such as but not limited to acting as base coach.

A DEAD BALL is a ball out of play because of a legally created temporary suspension of play.

The DEFENSE (or DEFENSIVE) is the team, or any player of the team, in the field.

A DOUBLE-HEADER is two regularly scheduled or rescheduled games, played in immediate succession.

A DOUBLE PLAY is a play by the defense in which two offensive players are put out as a result of continuous action, providing there is no error between putouts.

    (a) A force double play is one in which both putouts are force plays.

    (b) A reverse force double play is one in which the first out is made at first base and the second out is made by tagging a runner who originally was forced, before the runner touches the base to which he was forced.

A FAIR BALL is a batted ball that settles on fair ground between home and first base, or between home and third base, or that is on or over fair territory when bounding to the outfield past first or third base, or that touches first, second or third base, or that first falls on fair territory on or beyond first base or third base, or that, while on or over fair territory, touches the person of an umpire or player, or that, while over fair territory, passes out of the playing field in flight.

> NOTE: A fair fly shall be judged according to the relative position of the ball and the foul line, including the foul pole, and not as to whether the fielder is on fair or foul territory at the time he touches the ball.

FAIR TERRITORY is that part of the playing field within, and including the first base and third base lines, from home base to the bottom of the playing field fence and perpendicularly upwards. All foul lines are in fair territory.

A FIELDER is any defensive player.

FIELDER'S CHOICE is the act of a fielder who handles a fair grounder and, instead of throwing to first base to put out the batter-runner, throws to another base in an attempt to put out a preceding runner. The term is also used by scorers (a) to account for the advance of the batter-runner who takes one or more extra bases when the fielder who handles his safe hit attempts to put out a preceding runner; (b) to account for the advance of a runner (other than by stolen base or error) while a fielder is attempting to put out another runner; and (c) to account for the advance of a runner made solely because of the defensive team's indifference. (Undefended steal).

A FLY BALL is a batted ball that goes high in the air in flight.

A FORCE PLAY is a play in which a runner legally loses his right to occupy a base by reason of the batter becoming a runner.

A FORFEITED GAME is a game declared ended by the umpire-in-chief in favor of the offended team by the score of 9 to 0, for violation of the rules.

A FOUL BALL is a batted ball that settles on foul territory between home and first base, or between home and third base, or that bounds past first or third base on or over foul territory, or that first falls on foul territory beyond first or third base, or that, while on or over foul territory, touches the person of an umpire or player, or any object foreign to the natural ground.

> NOTE: A foul fly shall be judged according to the relative position of the ball and the foul line, including the foul pole, and not as to whether the fielder is on foul or fair territory at the time he touches the ball.

FOUL TERRITORY is that part of the playing field outside the first and third base lines extended to the fence and perpendicularly upwards.

A FOUL TIP is a batted ball that goes sharp and direct from the bat to the catcher's hands and is legally caught. It is not a foul tip unless caught and any foul tip that is caught is a strike, and the ball is in play. It is not a catch if it is a rebound, unless the ball has first touched the catcher's glove or hand.

A GROUND BALL is a batted ball that rolls or bounces close to the ground.

The HOME TEAM is the team on whose ground the game is played, or if the game is played on neutral grounds, the home team shall be designated by mutual agreement.

ILLEGAL (or ILLEGALLY) is contrary to these rules.

An ILLEGAL PITCH is (1) a pitch delivered to the batter when the pitcher does not have his pivot foot in contact with the pitcher's plate; (2) a pitch delivered in violation of Rule 8.02 (a) (5), or (3) a quick return pitch. An illegal pitch when runners are on base is a balk.

An ILLEGALLY BATTED BALL is (1) one hit by the batter with one or both feet on the ground entirely outside the batter's box, or (2) one hit with a bat which does not conform to Rule 1.10.

An INFIELDER is a fielder who occupies a position in the infield.

An INFIELD FLY is a fair fly ball (not including a line drive nor an attempted bunt) which can be caught by an infielder with ordinary effort, when first and second, or first, second and third bases are occupied, before two are out. The pitcher, catcher and any outfielder who stations himself in the infield on the play shall be considered infielders for the purpose of this rule.

When it seems apparent that a batted ball will be an Infield Fly, the umpire shall immediately declare "Infield Fly" for the benefit of the runners. If the ball is near the baselines, the umpire shall declare "Infield Fly, if Fair."

The ball is alive and runners may advance at the risk of the ball being caught, or retouch and advance after the ball is touched, the same as on any fly ball. If the hit becomes a foul ball, it is treated the same as any foul.

> NOTE: If a declared Infield Fly is allowed to fall untouched to the ground, and bounces foul before passing first or third base, it is a foul ball. If a declared Infield Fly falls untouched to the ground outside the baseline, and bounces fair before passing first or third base, it is an Infield Fly.

IN FLIGHT describes a batted, thrown, or pitched ball which has not yet touched the ground or some object other than a fielder.

IN JEOPARDY is a term indicating that the ball is in play and an offensive player may be put out.

An INNING is that portion of a game within which the teams alternate on offense and defense and in which there are three putouts for each team. Each team's time at bat is a half-inning.

INTERFERENCE

(a) Offensive interference is an act by the team at bat which interferes with, obstructs, impedes, hinders or confuses any fielder attempting to make a play. If the umpire declares the batter, batter-runner, or a runner out for interference, all other runners shall return to the last base that was, in the judgment of the umpire, legally touched at the time of the interference, unless otherwise provided by these rules.

(b) Defensive interference is an act by a fielder which hinders or prevents a batter from hitting a pitch.

(c) Umpire's interference occurs (1) When an umpire hinders, impedes or prevents a catcher's throw attempting to prevent a stolen base, or (2) When a fair ball touches an umpire on fair territory before passing a fielder.

(d) Spectator interference occurs when a spectator reaches out of the stands, or goes on the playing field, and touches a live ball.

On any interference the ball is dead.

LEGAL (or LEGALLY) is in accordance with these rules.

A LIVE BALL is a ball which is in play.

OBSTRUCTION is the act of a fielder who, while not in possession of the ball and not in the act of fielding the ball, impedes the progress of any runner.

OFFENSE is the team, or any player of the team, at bat.

An OUT is one of the three required retirements of an offensive team during its time at bat.

An OUTFIELDER is a fielder who occupies a position in the outfield, which is the area of the playing field most distant from home base.

OVERSLIDE (or OVERSLIDING) is the act of an offensive player when his slide to a base, other than when advancing from home to first base, is with such momentum that he loses contact with the base.

A PENALTY is the application of these rules following an illegal act.

The PERSON of a player or an umpire is any part of his body, his clothing or his equipment.

A PITCH is a ball delivered to the batter by the pitcher.

A PITCHER is the fielder designated to deliver the pitch to the batter.

The pitcher's PIVOT FOOT is that foot which is in contact with the pitcher's plate as he delivers the pitch.

"PLAY" is the umpire's order to start the game or to resume action following any dead ball.

A QUICK RETURN pitch is one made with obvious intent to catch a batter off balance. It is an illegal pitch.

A RETOUCH is the act of a runner in returning to a base as legally required.

A RUN (or SCORE) is the score made by an offensive player who advances from batter to runner and touches first, second, third and home bases in that order.

A RUNDOWN is the act of the defense in an attempt to put out a runner between bases.

A RUNNER is an offensive player who is advancing toward, or touching, or returning to any base.

"SAFE" is a declaration by the umpire that a runner is entitled to the base for which he was trying.

SET POSITION is one of the two legal pitching positions.

SQUEEZE PLAY is a term to designate a play when a team, with a runner on third base, attempts to score that runner by means of a bunt.

A STRIKE is a legal pitch when so called by the umpire, which—
(a) Is struck at by the batter and is missed;
(b) Is not struck at, if any part of the ball passes through any part of the strike zone;
(c) Is fouled by the batter when he has less than two strikes;
(d) Is bunted foul;
(e) Touches the batter as he strikes at it;
(f) Touches the batter in flight in the strike zone; or
(g) Becomes a foul tip.

The STRIKE ZONE is that space over home plate which is between the top of the batter's shoulders and his knees when he assumes his natural stance. The umpire shall determine the strike zone according to the batter's usual stance when he swings at a pitch.

A TAG is the action of a fielder in touching a base with his body while holding the ball securely and firmly in his hand or glove; or touching a runner with the ball, or with his hand or glove holding the ball, while holding the ball securely and firmly in his hand or glove.

A THROW is the act of propelling the ball with the hand and arm to a given objective and is to be distinguished, always, from the pitch.

A TIE GAME is a regulation game which is called when each team has the same number of runs.

"TIME" is the announcement by an umpire of a legal interruption of play, during which the ball is dead.

A TRIPLE PLAY is a play by the defense in which three offensive players are put out as a result of continuous action, providing there is no error between putouts.

A WILD PITCH is one so high, so low, or so wide of the plate that

it cannot be handled with ordinary effort by the catcher.
WIND-UP POSITION is one of the two legal pitching positions.

3.00—Game Preliminaries.

3.01 Before the game begins the umpire shall—
  (a) Require strict observance of all rules governing implements of play and equipment of players;
  (b) Be sure that all playing lines (heavy lines on Diagrams No. 1 and No. 2) are marked with lime, chalk or other white material easily distinguishable from the ground or grass;

3.02 No player shall intentionally discolor or damage the ball by rubbing it with soil, rosin, paraffin, licorice, sand-paper, emery-paper or other foreign substance.

> PENALTY: The umpire shall demand the ball and re-move the offender from the game. In case the umpire cannot locate the offender, and if the pitcher delivers such discolored or damaged ball to the batter, the pitcher shall be removed from the game at once and shall be suspended automatically for ten days.

3.16 When there is spectator interference with any thrown or batted ball, the ball shall be dead at the moment of interference and the umpire shall impose such penalties as in his opinion will nullify the act of interference.

> APPROVED RULING: If spectator interference clearly prevents a fielder from catching a fly ball, the umpire shall declare the batter out.

4.00—Starting and Ending a Game.

4.01 Unless the home club shall have given previous notice that the game has been postponed or will be delayed in starting, the umpire, or umpires, shall enter the playing field five minutes before the hour set for the game to begin and proceed directly to home base where they shall be met by the managers of the opposing teams.
In sequence—
  (a) First, the home manager shall give his batting order to the umpire-in-chief, in duplicate.
  (b) Next, the visiting manager shall give his batting order to the umpire-in-chief, in duplicate.
  (c) The umpire-in-chief shall make certain that the original and copies of the respective batting orders are identical, and then tender a copy of each batting order to the opposing manager. The copy retained by the umpire shall be the official batting order. The tender of the batting order by the umpire shall establish the batting orders. Thereafter, no substitutions shall be made by either manager, except as provided in these rules.
  (d) As soon as the home team's batting order is handed to the umpire-in-chief the umpires are in charge of the playing field and from that moment they shall have sole authority to determine when a game shall be called suspended, or resumed on account of weather or the condition of the playing field.

4.02 The players of the home team shall take their defensive positions, the first batter of the visiting team shall take his position in the batter's box, the umpire shall call "Play" and the game shall start.

4.09 HOW A TEAM SCORES.
  (a) One run shall be scored each time a runner legally advances to and touches first, second, third and home base before three men are put out to end the inning. EXCEPTION: A run is not scored if the runner advances to home base during a play in which the third out is made (1) by the batter-runner before he touches first base; (2) by any runner being forced out; or (3) by a preceding runner who is declared out because he failed to touch one of the bases.

(b) When the winning run is scored in the last half-inning of a regulation game, or in the last half of an extra inning, as the result of a base on balls, hit batter or any other play with the bases full which forces the runner on third to advance, the umpire shall not declare the game ended until the runner forced to advance from third has touched home base and the batter-runner has touched first base.

PENALTY: If the runner on third refuses to advance to and touch home base in a reasonable time, the umpire shall disallow the run, call out the offending player and order the game resumed. If, with two out, the batter-runner refuses to advance to and touch first base, the umpire shall disallow the run, call out the offending player, and order the game resumed. If, before two are out, the batter-runner refuses to advance to and touch first base, the run shall count, but the offending player shall be called out.

4.10 (a) A regulation game consists of nine innings, unless extended because of a tie score, or shortened (1) because the home team needs none of its half of the ninth inning or only a fraction of it, or (2) because the umpire calls the game. EXCEPTION: National Association leagues may adopt a rule providing that one or both games of a doubleheader shall be seven innings in length. In such games, any of these rules applying to the ninth inning shall apply to the seventh inning.

(b) If the score is tied after nine completed innings, play shall continue until (1) the visiting team has scored more total runs than the home team at the end of a completed inning, or (2) the home team scores the winning run in an uncompleted inning.

(c) If a game is called, it is a regulation game
(1) If five innings have been completed;
(2) If the home team has scored more runs in four or four and a fraction half-innings than the visiting team has scored in five completed half-innings;
(3) If the home team scores one or more runs in its half of the fifth inning to tie the score.

(d) If each team has the same number of runs when the tie game ends, the umpire shall declare it a "Tie Game."

(e) If a game is called before it has become a regulation game, the umpire shall declare it "No Game."

4.11 The score of a regulation game is the total number of runs scored by each team at the moment the game ends.

(a) The game ends when the visiting team completes its half of the ninth inning if the home team is ahead.

(b) The game ends when the ninth inning is completed, if the visiting team is ahead.

(c) If the home team scores the winning run in its half of the ninth inning (or its half of an extra inning after a tie), the game ends immediately when the winning run is scored. EXCEPTION: If the last batter in a game hits a home run out of the playing field, the batter-runner and all runners on base are permitted to score, in accordance with the base-running rules, and the game ends when the batter-runner touches home plate.

APPROVED RULING: PLAY (1) The batter hits a home run out of the playing field to win the game in the last half of the ninth or an extra inning, but is called out for passing a preceding runner. The game ends immediately when the winning run is scored.

(d) A called game ends at the moment the umpire terminates play. EXCEPTION: If the game is called during an uncompleted inning, the game ends at the end of the last previous completed inning in each of the following situations:

(1) The visiting team scores one or more runs to tie the score in the uncompleted inning, and the home team does not score;

(2) The visiting team scores one or more runs to take the lead in the uncompleted inning, and the home team does not tie the score or re-take the lead.

5.00—Ball in Play

5.09 The ball becomes dead and runners advance one base, or return to their bases, without liability to be put out, when—

(a) A pitched ball touches a batter, or his clothing, while in his legal batting position; runners, if forced, advance;

(b) The plate umpire interferes with the catcher's throw attempting to prevent a stolen base; runners return;

(c) A balk is committed; runners advance;

(d) A ball is illegally batted; runners return;

(e) A foul ball is not caught; runners return. The umpire shall not put the ball in play until all runners have retouched their bases;

(f) A fair ball touches a runner or an umpire on fair territory before it touches an infielder including the pitcher, or touches an umpire before it has passed an infielder other than the pitcher;

> NOTE: If a fair ball goes through, or by, an infielder, and touches a runner immediately back of him, or touches a runner after being deflected by an infielder, the ball is in play and the umpire shall not declare the runner out. In making such decision the umpire must be convinced that the ball passed through, or by, the infielder and that no other infielder had the chance to make a play on the ball; runners advance, if forced;

(g) A base coach intentionally interferes with a thrown ball; runners return;

(h) A pitched ball passes the catcher and lodges in the umpire's mask or paraphernalia; runners advance;

(i) Any legal pitch touches a runner trying to score; runners advance;

5.11 After the ball is dead, play shall be resumed when the pitcher takes his place on the pitcher's plate with a new ball or the same ball in his possession and the plate umpire calls "Play." The plate umpire shall call "Play" as soon as the pitcher takes his place on his plate with the ball in his possession.

6.00—The Batter

6.02 (a) The batter shall take his position in the batter's box promptly when it is his time at bat.

(b) The batter shall not leave his position in the batter's box after the pitcher comes to Set Position, or starts his windup.

> PENALTY: If the pitcher pitches, the umpire shall call "Ball" or "Strike," as the case may be.

(c) If the batter refuses to take his position in the batter's box during his time at bat, the umpire shall order the pitcher to pitch, and shall call "Strike" on each such pitch. The batter may take his proper position after any such pitch, and the regular ball and strike count shall continue, but if he does not take his proper position before three strikes are called, he shall be declared out.

6.03 The batter's legal position shall be with both feet within the batter's box.

> APPROVED RULING: The lines defining the box are within the batter's box.

6.04 A batter has legally completed his time at bat when he is put out or becomes a runner.

6.05 A batter is out when—

(a) His fair or foul fly ball (other than a foul tip) is legally caught by a fielder;

(b) A third strike is legally caught by the catcher;

(c) A third strike is not caught by the catcher when first base is occupied before two are out;

(d) He bunts foul on the third strike;

(e) An Infield Fly is declared;

(f) He attempts to hit a third strike and the ball touches him;

(g) His fair ball touches him before touching a fielder;

(h) After hitting or bunting a fair ball, his bat hits the ball a second time in fair territory. The ball is dead and no runners may advance. If the batter-runner drops his bat and the ball rolls against the bat in fair territory and, in the umpire's judgment, there was no intention to interfere with the course of the ball, the ball is alive and in play;

(i) After hitting or bunting a foul ball, he intentionally deflects the course of the ball in any manner while running to first base. The ball is dead and no runners may advance;

(j) After a third strike or after he hits a fair ball, he or first base is tagged before he touches first base;

(k) In running the last half of the distance from home base to first base, while the ball is being fielded to first base, he runs outside (to the right of) the three-foot line, or inside (to the left of) the foul line, and in the umpire's judgment in so doing interferes with the fielder taking the throw at first base; except that he may run outside (to the right of) the three-foot line or inside (to the left of) the foul line to avoid a fielder attempting to field a batted ball;

(l) A fielder intentionally drops a fair fly ball or line drive, with first, first and second, first and third, or first, second and third base occupied before two are out. Runners need not retouch, and may advance at their own peril;

> APPROVED RULING: In this situation, the batter is not out if the fielder permits the ball to drop untouched to the ground, except when the Infield Fly rule applies.

(m) A preceding runner shall, in the umpire's judgment, intentionally interfere with a fielder who is attempting to catch a thrown ball or to throw a ball in an attempt to complete any play;

(n) With two out, a runner on third base, and two strikes on the batter, the runner attempts to steal home base on a legal pitch and the ball touches the runner in the batter's strike zone. The umpire shall call "Strike Three," the batter is out and the run shall not count; before two are out, the umpire shall call "Strike Three," the ball is dead, and the run counts.

6.06 A batter is out for illegal action when—

(a) He hits an illegally batted ball;

(b) He steps from one batter's box to the other while the pitcher is in position ready to pitch;

(c) He interferes with the catcher's fielding or throwing by stepping out of the batter's box or making any other movement that hinders the catcher's play at home base. EXCEPTION: Batter is not out if any runner attempting to advance is put out, or if runner trying to score is called out for batter's interference.

6.07 BATTING OUT OF TURN.

(a) A batter shall be called out, on appeal, when he fails to bat in his proper turn, and another batter completes a time at bat in his place.

(1) The proper batter may take his place in the batter's box at any time before the improper batter becomes a runner or is put out, and any balls and strikes shall be counted in the proper batter's time at bat.

(b) When an improper batter becomes a runner or is put out, and the defensive team appeals to the umpire before the first pitch to the next batter of either team, or before any play or attempted play, the umpire shall (1) declare the proper batter out; and (2) nullify any advance or score made because of a ball batted by the improper batter or because of the improper batter's advance to first base on a hit, an error, a base on balls, a hit batter or otherwise.

> NOTE: If a runner advances, while the improper batter is at bat, on a stolen base, balk, wild pitch or passed ball, such advance is legal.

(c) When an improper batter becomes a runner or is put out, and a pitch is made to the next batter of either team before an appeal is made, the improper batter thereby becomes the proper batter, and the results of his time at bat become legal.

(d) (1) When the proper batter is called out because he has failed to bat in turn, the next batter shall be the batter whose name follows that of the proper batter thus called out; (2) When an improper batter becomes a proper batter because no appeal is made before the next pitch, the next batter shall be the batter whose name follows that of such legalized improper batter. The instant an improper batter's actions are legalized, the batting order picks up with the name following that of the improper legalized batter.

6.08 The batter becomes a runner and is entitled to first base without liability to be put out (provided he advances to and touches first base) when—

(a) Four "balls" have been called by the umpire;

(b) He is touched by a pitched ball which he is not attempting to hit unless (1) The ball is in the strike zone when it touches the batter, or (2) The batter makes no attempt to avoid being touched by the ball;

> NOTE: If the ball is in the strike zone when it touches the batter, it shall be called a strike, whether or not the batter tries to avoid the ball. If the ball is outside the strike zone when it touches the batter, it shall be called a ball if he makes no attempt to avoid being touched.

> APPPROVED RULING: When the batter is touched by a pitched ball which does not entitle him to first base, the ball is dead and no runner may advance.

(c) The catcher or any fielder interferes with him. If a play follows the interference, the manager of the offense may advise the plate umpire that he elects to decline the interference penalty and accept the play. Such election shall be made immediately at the end of the play. However, if the batter reaches first base on a hit, an error, a base on balls, a hit batsman, or otherwise, and all other runners advance at least one base, the play proceeds without reference to the interference.

(d) A fair ball touches an umpire or a runner on fair territory before touching a fielder.

> NOTE: If a fair ball touches an umpire after having passed a fielder other than the pitcher, or having touched a fielder, including the pitcher, the ball is in play.

6.09 The batter becomes a runner when—

(a) He hits a fair ball;

(b) The third strike called by the umpire is not caught, providing

(1) first base is unoccupied, or (2) first base is occupied with two out;

(c) A fair ball, after having passed a fielder other than the pitcher, or after having been touched by a fielder, shall touch an umpire or runner on fair territory;

(d) A fair fly ball passes over a fence or into the stands at a distance from home base of 250 feet or more. Such hit entitles the batter to a home run when he shall have touched all bases legally. A fair fly ball that passes out of the playing field at a point less than 250 feet from home base shall entitle the batter to advance to second base only;

(e) A fair ball, after touching the ground, bounds into the stands, or passes through, over or under a fence, or through or under a scoreboard, or through or under shrubbery, or vines on the fence, in which case the batter and the runners shall be entitled to advance two bases;

(f) Any fair ball which, either before or after touching the ground, passes through or under a fence, or through or under a scoreboard, or through any opening in the fence or scoreboard, or through or under shrubbery, or vines on the fence, or which sticks in a fence or scoreboard, in which case the batter and the runners shall be entitled to two bases;

(g) Any bounding fair ball is deflected by the fielder into the stands, or over or under a fence on fair or foul territory, in which case the batter and all runners shall be entitled to advance two bases;

(h) Any fair fly ball is deflected by the fielder into the stands, or over the fence into foul territory, in which case the batter shall be entitled to advance to second base; but if deflected into the stands or over the fence in fair territory, the batter shall be entitled to a home run. However, should such fair fly be deflected at a point less than 250 feet from home plate, the batter shall be entitled to two bases only.

7.00—The Runner.

7.01 A runner acquires the right to an unoccupied base when he touches it before he is out. He is then entitled to it until he is put out, or forced to vacate it for another runner.

7.02 In advancing, a runner shall touch first, second, third and home base in order. If forced to return, he shall retouch all bases in reverse order, unless the ball is dead under any provision of Rule 5.09. In such cases, the runner may go directly to his original base.

7.03 Two runners may not occupy a base, but if, while the ball is alive, two runners are touching a base, the following runner shall be out when tagged. The preceding runner is entitled to the base.

7.04 Each runner, other than the batter, may without liability to be put out, advance one base when—

(a) There is a balk;

(b) The batter's advance without liability to be put out forces the runner to vacate his base, or when the batter hits a fair ball that touches another runner or the umpire before such ball has been touched by, or has passed a fielder, if the runner is forced to advance.

(c) A fielder, after catching a fly ball, falls into a bench or stand, or falls across ropes into a crowd when spectators are on the field;

(d) While he is attempting to steal a base, the batter is interfered with by the catcher or any other fielder.

NOTE: When a runner is entitled to a base without liability to be put out, while the ball is in play, or under any rule in which the ball is in play after the runner reaches the base to which he is entitled, and the runner fails to touch the base to which he is entitled before attempting to advance to the next base, the runner shall forfeit his exemption from liability to be put out, and he may be put out by tagging the base or by tagging the runner before he returns to the missed base.

7.05 Each runner including the batter-runner may, without liability to be put out, advance—

(a) To home base, scoring a run, if a fair ball goes out of the playing field in flight and he touches all bases legally; or if a fair ball which, in the umpire's judgment, would have gone out of the playing field in flight, is deflected by the act of a fielder in throwing his glove, cap, or any article of his apparel;

(b) Three bases, if a fielder deliberately touches a fair ball with his cap, mask or any part of his uniform detached from its proper place on his person. The ball is in play and the batter may advance to home base at his peril;

(c) Three bases, if a fielder deliberately throws his glove at and touches a fair ball. The ball is in play and the batter may advance to home base at his peril;

(d) Two bases, if a fielder deliberately touches a thrown ball with his cap, mask or any part of his uniform detached from its proper place on his person. The ball is in play;

(e) Two bases, if a fielder deliberately throws his glove at and touches a thrown ball. The ball is in play;

(f) Two bases, if a fair ball bounces or is deflected into the stands outside the first or third base foul lines; or if it goes through or under a field fence, or through or under a score-board, or through or under shrubbery or vines on the fence; or if it sticks in such fence, scoreboard, shrubbery or vines;

(g) Two bases when, with no spectators on the playing field, a thrown ball goes into the stands, or into a bench (whether or not the ball rebounds into the field), or over or under or through a field fence, or on a slanting part of the screen above the backstop, or remains in the meshes of a wire screen protecting spectators. The ball is dead. When such wild throw is the first play by an infielder, the umpire, in awarding such bases, shall be governed by the position of the runners at the time the ball was pitched; in all other cases the umpire shall be governed by the position of the runners at the time the wild throw was made;

APPROVED RULING: If all runners, including the batter-runner, have advanced at least one base when an infielder makes a wild throw on the first play after the pitch, the award shall be governed by the position of the runners when the wild throw was made.

(h) One base, if a ball, pitched to the batter, or thrown by the pitcher from his position on the pitcher's plate to a base to catch a runner, goes into a stand or a bench, or over or through a field fence or backstop. The ball is dead;

(i) One base, if the batter becomes a runner on Ball Four or Strike Three, when the pitch passes the catcher and lodges in the umpire's mask or paraphernalia.

NOTE: If the batter becomes a runner on a wild pitch which entitles the runners to advance one base, the batter-runner shall be entitled to first base only.

7.06 When obstruction occurs, the umpire shall call or signal "Obstruction."

(a) If a play is being made on the obstructed runner, or if the batter-runner is obstructed before he touches first base, the ball is dead and all runners shall advance, without liability to be put out, to the bases they would have reached, in the umpire's judgment, if there had been no obstruction. The obstructed runner shall be awarded at least one base beyond the base he had last legally touched before the obstruction. Any preceding runners, forced to advance by the award of bases as the penalty for obstruction, shall advance without liability to be put out.

(b) If no play is being made on the obstructed runner, the play shall proceed until no further action is possible. The umpire shall then call "Time" and impose such penalties, if any, as in his judgment will nullify the act of obstruction.

7.07 If, with a runner on third base and trying to score by means of a squeeze play or a steal, the catcher or any other fielder steps on, or in front of home base without possession of the ball, or touches the batter or his bat, the pitcher shall be charged with a balk, the batter shall be awarded first base on the interference and the ball is dead.

7.08 Any runner is out when—

(a) (1) He runs more than three feet away from a direct line between bases to avoid being tagged, unless his action is to avoid interference with a fielder fielding a batted ball; or (2) after touching first base, he leaves the baseline, obviously abandoning his effort to touch the next base;

APPROVED RULING: When a batter becomes a runner on third strike not caught, and starts for his bench or position, he may advance to first base at any time before he enters the bench. To put him out, the defense must tag him or first base before he touches first base.

(b) He intentionally interferes with a thrown ball; or hinders a fielder attempting to make a play on a batted ball;

(c) He is tagged, when the ball is alive, while off his base. EXCEPTION: A batter-runner cannot be tagged out after over-running or over-sliding first base if he returns immediately to the base;

APPROVED RULING: (1) If the impact of a runner breaks a base loose from its position, no play can be made on that runner at that base if he had reached the base safely.

APPROVED RULING: (2) If a base is dislodged from its position during a play, any following runner on the same play shall be considered as touching or occupying the base if, in the umpire's judgment, he touches or occupies the point marked by the dislodged bag.

(d) He fails to retouch his base after a fair or foul ball is legally caught before he, or his base, is tagged by a fielder. He shall not be called out for failure to retouch his base after the first following pitch. This is an appeal play;

(e) He fails to reach the next base before a fielder tags him or the base, after he has been forced to advance by reason of the batter becoming a runner. However, if a following runner is put out on a force play, the force is removed and the runner must be tagged to be put out. The force is removed as soon as the runner touches the base to which he is forced to advance, and if he overslides or overruns the base, the runner must be tagged to be put out. However, if the forced runner, after touching the next base, retreats for any reason towards the base he had last occupied, the force play is reinstated, and he can again be put out if the defense tags the base to which he is forced;

(f) He is touched by a fair ball in fair territory before the ball has touched or passed an infielder. The ball is dead and no runner may score, nor runners advance, except runners forced to advance. EXCEPTION: If a runner is touching his base when touched by an Infield Fly, he is not out, although the batter is out;

> NOTE: If runner is touched by an Infield Fly when he is not touching his base, both runner and batter are out.

(g) He attempts to score on a play in which the batter interferes with the play at home base before two are out. With two out, the interference puts the batter out and no score counts;

(h) He passes a preceding runner before such runner is out;

(i) After he has acquired legal possession of a base, he runs the bases in reverse order for the purpose of confusing the defense or making a travesty of the game. The umpire shall immediately call "Time" and declare the runner out;

(j) He fails to return at once to first base after overrunning or oversliding that base. If he attempts to run to second he is out when tagged. If, after overrunning or oversliding first base he starts toward the dugout, or toward his position, and fails to return to first base at once, he is out, on appeal, when he or the base is tagged;

(k) In running or sliding for home base, he fails to touch home base and makes no attempt to return to the base, when a fielder holds the ball in his hand, while touching home base, and appeals to the umpire for the decision.

7.09 It is interference by a batter or a runner when—

(a) After a third strike he hinders the catcher in his attempt to field the ball;

(b) After hitting or bunting a fair ball, his bat hits the ball a second time in fair territory. The ball is dead and no runners may advance. If the batter-runner drops his bat and the ball rolls against the bat in fair territory and, in the umpire's judgment, there was no intention to interfere with the course of the ball, the ball is alive and in play;

(c) He intentionally deflects the course of a foul ball in any manner;

(d) Before two are out and a runner on third base, the batter hinders a fielder in making a play at home base; the runner is out;

(e) Any member or members of the offensive team stand or gather around any base to which a runner is advancing, to confuse, hinder or add to the difficulty of the fielders. Such runner shall be declared out for the interference of his teammate or teammates;

(f) Any batter or runner who has just been put out hinders or impedes any following play being made on a runner. Such runner shall be declared out for the interference of his teammate;

(g) If, in the judgment of the umpire, a base runner wilfully and deliberately interferes with a batted ball or a fielder in the act of fielding a batted ball with the obvious intent to break up a double play, the ball is dead. The umpire shall call the runner out for interference and also call out the batter-runner because of the action of his teammate. In no event may bases be run or runs scored because of such action by a runner.

(h) If a batter-runner wilfully and deliberately interferes with a batted ball or a fielder in the act of fielding a batted ball, with the obvious intent to break up a double play, the ball is dead; the umpire shall call the batter-runner out for interference and shall also call out the runner who had advanced closest to the home plate regardless where the double play might have been possible. In no event shall bases be run because of such interference.

(i) In the judgment of the umpire, the base coach at third base, or first base, by touching or holding the runner, physically assists him in returning to or leaving third base or first base. The runner, however, shall not be declared out if no play is being made on him;

(j) With a runner on third base, the base coach leaves his box and acts in any manner to draw a throw by a fielder;

(k) In running the last half of the distance from home base to first base while the ball is being fielded to first base, he runs outside (to the right of) the three-foot line, or inside (to the left of) the foul line and, in the umpire's judgment, interferes with the fielder taking the throw at first base, or attempting to field a batted ball;

(l) He fails to avoid a fielder who is attempting to field a batted ball, or intentionally interferes with a thrown ball, provided that if two or more fielders attempt to field a batted ball, and the runner comes in contact with one or more of them, the umpire shall determine which fielder is entitled to the benefit of this rule, and shall not declare the runner out for coming in contact with a fielder other than the one the umpire determines to be entitled to field such a ball;

(m) A fair ball touches him on fair territory before touching a fielder. If a fair ball goes through, or by, an infielder, and touches a runner immediately back of him, or touches the runner after having been deflected by a fielder, the umpire shall not declare the runner out for being touched by a batted ball. In making such decision the umpire must be convinced that the ball passed through, or by, the infielder, and that no other infielder had the chance to make a play on the ball. If, in the judgment of the umpire, the runner deliberately and intentionally kicks such a batted ball on which the infielder has missed a play, then the runner shall be called out for interference.

PENALTY FOR INTERFERENCE: The runner is out and the ball is dead.

7.10 Any runner shall be called out, on appeal, when—

(a) After a fly ball is caught, he fails to re-touch his base before he or his base is tagged;

(b) With the ball in play, while advancing or returning to a base, he fails to touch each base in order before he, or a missed base, is tagged;

APPROVED RULING: (1) No runner may return to touch a missed base after a following runner has scored. (2) When the ball is dead, no runner may return to touch a missed base or one he has left after he has advanced to and touched a base beyond the missed base.

(c) He overruns or overslides first base and fails to return to the base immediately, and he or the base is tagged;

(d) He fails to touch home base and makes no attempt to return to that base, and home base is tagged.

Any appeal under this rule must be made before the next pitch, or any play or attempted play. If the violation occurs during a play which ends a half-inning, the appeal must be made before the defensive team leaves the field.

NOTE: Appeal plays may require an umpire to recognize an apparent "fourth out." If the third out is made during a play in which an appeal play is sustained on another runner, the appeal play decision takes precedence in determining the out. If there is more than one appeal during a play that ends a half-inning, the defense may elect to take the out that gives it the advantage. For the purposes of this rule, the defensive team has "left the field" when the pitcher and all infielders have left fair territory on their way to the bench or clubhouse.

7.11 The players or coaches of an offensive team shall vacate any space needed by a fielder who is attempting to field a batted or thrown ball.

> PENALTY: Interference shall be called and the batter or runner on whom the play is being made shall be declared out.

7.12 Unless two are out, the status of a following runner is not affected by a preceding runner's failure to touch or retouch a base. If, upon appeal, the preceding runner is the third out, no runners following him shall score. If such third out is the result of a force play, neither preceding nor following runners shall score.

8.00—The Pitcher.

8.01 Legal pitching delivery. There are two legal pitching positions, the Windup Position and the Set Position, and either position may be used at any time.

(a) The Windup Position. The pitcher shall stand facing the batter, his entire pivot foot on, or in front of and touching and not off the end of the pitcher's plate, and the other foot free. From this position any natural movement associated with his delivery of the ball to the batter commits him to the pitch without interruption or alteration. He shall not raise either foot from the ground, except that in his actual delivery of the ball to the batter, he may take one step backward, and one step forward with his free foot.

> NOTE: When a pitcher holds the ball with both hands in front of his body, with his entire pivot foot on, or in front of and touching but not off the end of the pitcher's plate, and his other foot free, he will be considered in a Windup Position.

(b) The Set Position. Set Position shall be indicated by the pitcher when he stands facing the batter with his entire pivot foot on, or in front of, and in contact with, and not off the end of the pitcher's plate, and his other foot in front of the pitcher's plate, holding the ball in both hands in front of his body and coming to a complete stop. From such Set Position he may deliver the ball to the batter, throw to a base or step backward off the pitcher's plate with his pivot foot. Before assuming Set Position, the pitcher may elect to make any natural preliminary motion such as that known as "the stretch." But if he so elects, he shall come to Set Position before delivering the ball to the batter. After assuming Set Position, any natural motion associated with his delivery of the ball to the batter commits him to the pitch without alteration or interruption.

(c) At any time during the pitcher's preliminary movements and until his natural pitching motion commits him to the pitch, he may throw to any base provided he steps directly toward such base before making the throw.

(d) If the pitcher makes an illegal pitch with the bases unoccupied, it shall be called a ball unless the batter reaches first base on a hit, an error, a base on balls, a hit batter or otherwise.

(e) If the pitcher removes his pivot foot from contact with the pitcher's plate by stepping backward with that foot, he thereby becomes an infielder and if he makes a wild throw from that position, it shall be considered the same as a wild throw by any other infielder.

8.02 The pitcher shall not—
   (a) (1) Apply a foreign substance of any kind to the ball; (2) expectorate either on the ball or his glove; (3) rub the ball on his glove, person or clothing; (4) deface the ball in any manner; (5) deliver what is called the "shine" ball, "spit" ball, "mud" ball or "emery" ball. The pitcher, of course, is allowed to rub the ball between his bare hands.

   PENALTY: For violation of any part of this rule the umpire shall immediately disoualify the pitcher.

   (b) Intentionally delay the game by throwing the ball to players other than the catcher, when the batter is in position, except in an attempt to retire a runner.

   PENALTY: If, after warning by the umpire, such delaying action is repeated, the pitcher shall be removed from the game.

   (c) Intentionally pitch at the batter. If, in the umpire's judgment, such violation occurs, the umpire shall warn the pitcher and the manager of the defense that another such pitch will mean immediate expulsion of the pitcher. If such pitch is repeated during the game, the umpire shall eject the pitcher from the game.

8.04 When the bases are unoccupied, the pitcher shall deliver the ball to the batter within 20 seconds after he receives the ball. Each time the pitcher delays the game by violating this rule, the umpire shall call "Ball."

   NOTE: The intent of this rule is to avoid unnecessary delays. The umpire shall insist that the catcher return the ball promptly to the pitcher, and that the pitcher take his position on the rubber promptly. Obvious delay by the pitcher should instantly be penalized by the umpire.

8.05 If there is a runner, or runners, it is a balk when—
   (a) The pitcher, while touching his plate, makes any motion naturally associated with his pitch and fails to make such delivery;
   (b) The pitcher, while touching his plate, feints a throw to first base and fails to complete the throw;
   (c) The pitcher, while touching his plate, fails to step directly toward a base before throwing to that base;
   (d) The pitcher, while touching his plate, throws, or feints a throw to an unoccupied base, except for the purpose of making a play;
   (e) The pitcher makes an illegal pitch;
   (f) The pitcher delivers the ball to the batter while he is not facing the batter;
   (g) The pitcher makes any motion naturally associated with his pitch while he is not touching the pitcher's plate;
   (h) The pitcher unnecessarily delays the game;
   (i) The pitcher, without having the ball, stands on or astride the pitcher's plate or while off the plate, he feints a pitch;
   (j) The pitcher, after coming to a legal pitching position, removes one hand from the ball other than - in an actual pitch, or in throwing to a base;
   (k) The pitcher, while touching his plate, accidentally or intentionally drops the ball;
   (l) The pitcher, while giving an intentional base on balls, pitches when the catcher is not in the catcher's box;
   (m) The pitcher delivers the pitch from Set Position without coming to a stop.

PENALTY: The ball is dead, and each runner shall advance one base without liability to be put out, unless the batter reaches first on a hit, an error, a base on balls, a hit batter, or otherwise, and all other runners advance at least one base, in which case the play proceeds without reference to the balk.

APPROVED RULING: A runner who misses the first base to which he is advancing and who is called out on appeal shall be considered as having advanced one base for the purpose of this rule.